Introduction

Everyone has had the experience of working for a not-so-great boss. While it's common for people to be promoted into management when they excel in non-leadership positions, the truth is that a lot of the people who get those promotions don't have the skills they need to effectively manage their team.

In other words, they lack the **must-have leadership skills** that all great bosses have in common.

The good news is that they're skills you can easily learn. In this special report, I'll explain the five essential leadership skills you need to successfully manage a team, and how to set yourself up for long-term success.

These critical steps include: communication, adaptability, team building, strategic thinking, and delegation.

Table of Contents

Are you ready to learn what it takes to become an effective leader? Let's get started!

Skill 1: Communication

Without proper, clear and concise communication, you can't hope to become an effective leader.

Communication is your best tool for explaining your ideas, setting expectations, and building your team. In this chapter, we'll talk about why strong communication skills are essential for leaders and share some tips about how to communicate effectively both in writing and in person.

The Importance of Interpersonal Communication

Interpersonal communication is what builds relationships. If you listen to employees complain about their bosses and employers, one of the top issues they're dealing with is usually lack of a direct and clear channel of communication.

Of course, communication goes both ways. But, as a leader, it's your job to set the tone for interaction within your organization or team.

Effective communication:

- Minimizes misunderstandings and confusion
- Ensures that team members know what you expect
- Encourages communication among team members
- Increases the chances that you'll reach your goals

Any time you touch base with your team or with a client, you're using communication skills. That means every phone call, every meeting, every chat, and every email reflects your ability to communicate and keep a pulse on how projects are going.

Tips for Effective Communication in Writing and Off the Cuff

What makes for effective communication? The hallmarks of a good communication are clarity, detail, and honesty.

Clarity means that you must be able to articulate what you want in a way that the person you're talking to can understand. You're not communicating effectively if the listener or reader can't understand what you need or expect from them.

Detail means that you are specific about what you want, expect, or need to know. If you delegate a task and the team member still has questions about what to do or how to do the job, your communication skills have fallen short.

Honesty means that you must be truthful when communicating with your team. That doesn't mean you need to tell them everything you're thinking all the time, but it does mean that you cannot mislead them or deliberately omit information that might help them achieve the goals you've laid out for the team.

Here are a few tips for communicating effectively:

- In writing, keep your sentences and paragraphs short

- Think about what you say before you say it

- Always keep your audience in mind. Don't use jargon unless you're sure they'll understand it

- Pay attention to how the listener reacts to what you say

- Be available to answer questions and patient while you do it

These tips will help you be an effective communicator and enhance your ability to lead.

Coming up next, we'll talk about why you must be adaptable if you want to become a great leader.

Skill 2: Adaptability

You've heard about survival of the fittest. It's the principle that tells us that only those who can handle change and cope with adversity survive. In other words, adaptability is necessary – and it can mean the difference between success and failure in your business.

In this chapter, we'll talk about why great leaders must be adaptable, and provide some tips about how you can increase your adaptability and learn to go with the flow.

How Adaptability Can Help You Succeed

In our professional lives, things seldom go the way we want them to. There are too many variables for that to always be the case and often, the things that derail our career or our personal lives feels as though it's out of our control.

There have been many times in my life when I've had an expectation that hasn't been met – and I'm willing to bet that's true for you, too.

The bottom line is that what you do in the face of adversity is what'll determine whether you're able to quickly recover, reset and get back on the path to success.

If you have a setback, do you get up and keep going – or do you give up and move onto something else?

Great leaders learn to go with the flow. They understand that success doesn't happen overnight. Their adaptability helps them get through failure and come out the other side a winner.

Tips for Increasing Adaptability and Going with the Flow

Some people have a high level of adaptability naturally. If that's you, then you're probably in good shape.

But what if it's not? What if you're easily discouraged or daunted by setbacks? Is there anything you can do to increase your adaptability?

Yes!

Here are some tips to help you increase your adaptability and go with the flow.

1. Make contingency plans. You should always have a Plan B. It doesn't mean you're planning for failure. Instead, it means that you've given thought to what you'll do if Plan A doesn't go as planned.

2. Practice resilience. If you're like most people, you probably experience tons of small setbacks. When one happens, pay attention to how you react and think about how you can switch up your internal monologue to be more positive.

3. Come up with a daily affirmation to remind yourself that you can deal with disappointment. You might try something like, "Even if things don't go my way today, I'm going to keep going and not get bogged down by it."

4. When something goes wrong, don't react immediately. Take a few deep breaths and let yourself feel the disappointment. A lot of times, we get wrapped up in disappointment because we're trying to hard to overcome it. It's okay to feel disappointed – but it's not okay to let it get the best of you.

These tips can help you learn to be more resilient. Even a big disappointment or a disappointing failure doesn't have to mean that your goals are out of reach.

Coming up next, we'll talk about how to build a team – something that's very important for every leader. Keep reading to learn more!

Skill 3: Team Building

We'll always reach a higher level of success with a team. Even the self-made millionaires and billionaires out there didn't do it entirely on their own. Bill Gates is a great example. Yes, he had a great idea when he created Windows – but he had a talented team of programmers, designers, writers, marketers, and administrators to help him launch it.

In this chapter, we'll talk about why team-building is an essential leadership skill, and how you can recognize the areas where you need help so you can build a powerhouse team of your own.

The Benefits of Building a Strong Team

As hard as you may work and as determined as you may be, you can't do everything on your own, nor should you. It's not practical, and it's not working smarter – it's working harder.

Consider the phrase, "Jack of all trades, master of none." You might be great at some things, but chances are there are areas in your business that would benefit from outside support.

You might be tempted to try to do everything yourself, telling yourself that you'll save money. A lot of entrepreneurs make that mistake and it leads to failure. They undervalue their time and energy and underestimate how hard it will be to wear every hat, every day.

Choosing a team means that you'll have ongoing support within your own customized network. You can delegate tasks – something we'll talk about later – and have time to do the things you do best. You'll also be able to enjoy other aspects of life because, let's face it, you'll work better if you make time to play, too.

The trick, of course, is building the right team.

Tips for Attracting Team Members and Knowing When You Need Help

You need a team, but where you do you start?

The first step is identifying the key areas where you need help. If you're building a business, you'll need to build a brand, create products, design your website, structure mailing lists, attract new clients, service those clients, and so on.

Start by looking at the things you do very well. Maybe you're a killer salesperson or a master communicator. Those may be things you can do on your own.

Next, look at the things that aren't in your wheelhouse. Maybe you have very little marketing experience or you're not great at organization.

The first team members you hire should be the people who can help you with your weaknesses. You'll have the best chance of success if you use this method.

The next thing you need to do is attract the right team members.

To do that, you'll need to:

- Write accurate and attractive job descriptions.
- Offer fair payment.
- Place ads to help team members find you or look for them on sites like LinkedIn.
- Interview people.

Make sure that you ask for samples of their work where it's appropriate and check their references. These days, it's easy to hire people to work remotely without ever meeting them. You should set up Skype interviews with anyone you don't plan to meet in person.

It's also a good idea to impose a probation period on any new hires. That way, you'll be able to make changes easily if you need to. Just make sure to put everything in writing.

Next, we'll talk about strategic thinking.

Skill 4: Strategic Thinking

Strategy thinking is *an essential element of leadership*. In this chapter, I'll explain why and give you some tips for improving your strategic thinking and planning skills.

The Role of Strategy in Success

Strategy is simply **long-term planning** with a fancy name. You have a goal in mind and then you map out a step-by-step plan to achieve it. If you want it to work, your strategy must be logical and practical. Each step you take should build to the next step.

Without strategy, it's very difficult – maybe even impossible – to achieve your biggest goals. You might have the goal to be the CEO of a Fortune 500 company. Your strategy might include getting an MBA and a host of other steps that will put you in a position to achieve that goal.

The thing about strategy is that it's not just for you. Having a strategy in place can help you get investors to fund your company, and it can also help you inspire your team.

Tips for Improving Your Strategic Thinking and Planning Ahead

Some people have a natural gift for strategic thinking. They're the people who are great chess players and who naturally seem to see everything 10 steps ahead.

If you're not one of them, don't worry. Here are some tips to help you improve your strategic thinking.

■ Before you make any decision, think about some possible outcomes and brainstorm what you'll do next with each one. This is the kind of practical thinking that can help you become a better strategist.

- Think about your goals and work backwards to figure out what actions will help you achieve them. Think of this as reverse-engineering a strategy.

- Ask team members and trusted friends for suggestions to help you plan strategically.

- Try creating a timeline to plan each step on the way to your goal.

The more you practice strategic thinking, the easier it will be.

Coming up next, we'll talk about the fifth and final must-have leadership skill in this book: delegation.

Skill 5: Delegation

In some ways, delegation is the most important skill of them all. I've already touched on some reasons why it's important not to try to do everything yourself. The key to making that happen is to learn how to delegate effectively.

In this chapter, we'll talk about why delegation is important and provide some tips to help you delegate the right tasks to the right people.

Why You Shouldn't Try to Do Everything Yourself

If you want to be a great leader, you need to know how to delegate tasks and – just as importantly – *who* to delegate them to.

You might have a ton of energy and the will to do everything yourself, but as I said before, it's not always an effective strategy.

Not only will you be shouldering the responsibility for tasks that aren't in your wheelhouse, but you also run the risk of burning out.

We all need down time – and we all do our best work when we're focused on what we're good at and love to do. Delegation allows you to focus your time and energy on the things you're best it and the things that only you can do.

That means you'll have more time to lead because you won't be burned out from trying to do everything.

Tips to Help You Decide What to Delegate to Others

The trick to great delegation is knowing two things:

1. Which tasks and jobs can be delegated; and
2. Who should handle those tasks.

So, let's take each of these things in turn, starting with knowing which tasks to delegate. You should delegate:

- Things that your team members excel at
- Things they can be taught to do
- Things that don't require your personal input

It might be useful to start by identifying the things that only you can do. These may include making strategic decisions about your team or meeting with investors.

Then, make a list of the things you can delegate. Once you've got the list, it's time to think about who the best people are for those jobs. Here are some questions to ask:

- Which team members already have skills that make them suitable for the task?
- Which team members have shown aptitude for core skills, like communication, teamwork, or logic?

- Which team members are eager to learn and willing to take on something new?

Any of these questions can help you identify people who are ready to handle the tasks and responsibilities you've identified.

Once you've identified the people you need, you should spend some time thinking about the training and support they'll need to succeed with their delegated tasks. You may need to spend some one-on-one time with them or pay someone else to train them. They may need an outside class or seminar.

Delegate the tasks, and make sure that you communicate clearly and in detail about what you expect from each team member.

Make yourself available to answer questions, and most importantly, keep in mind that they may not get it right on the first try.

There's a chance that you may need to adapt along the way. You might not pick the best team member for every task on your first try. The key is to keep an open mind, listen, and be patient.

You'll need all your leadership skills to decide what to delegate, choose the best people for each job, and guide them along the way to success. That's why I saved delegation for last – because it's a skill that necessarily incorporates all the others we've discussed.

Final Words

Thank you for reading *Follow the Leader: 5 Must-Have Leadership Skills*! I hope you've found the information in this special report to be enlightening, useful, and inspiring.

As a reminder, here are some core concepts to remember as you work to build your leadership skills:

1. Practice communication all the time and be willing to learn from your mistakes. Remember that all communication should be done with clarity, detail, and honesty.
2. Improve your adaptability by reminding yourself that you can handle disappointment and by learning to make contingency plans.
3. Build your team by recognizing the danger of trying to do everything yourself and choosing team members who have the skills and experience you lack.

4. Learn how to think strategically by outlining your goals and identifying the practical steps you need to take to achieve them.

5. Delegate skills by assigning the tasks that don't require your personal attention to the team members best suited to do them.

Some so-called experts treat leadership like it's a riddle to be solved. I don't think of it that way. It's a skill – or rather a set of skills – that anybody can acquire if they're willing to do the work.

The five core skills I've described in this book can be the basis of great leadership. I believe you can be a great leader – and you should too!

Good luck!

www.ingramcontent.com/pod-product-compliance
Lightning Source LLC
Chambersburg PA
CBHW080232180526
45158CB00010BA/3156